Finding Shapes with Sebastian Pig and Friends At the Museum

By Jill Anderson

Illustrated by Amy Huntington

Series Math Consultant:
Cassi Heppelmann
Elementary School Teacher
Farmington School District
Minnesota

Series Literacy Consultant:
Allan A. De Fina, Ph.D.
Dean, College of Education / Professor of Literacy Education
New Jersey City University
Past President of the New Jersey Reading Association

Enslow Elementary
an imprint of
Enslow Publishers, Inc.

E

40 Industrial Road
Box 398
Berkeley Heights, NJ 07922
USA

http://www.enslow.com

To Parents and Teachers:

As you read Sebastian's story with a child,

*Rely on the pictures to see the math visually represented.

*Use Sebastian's notebook, which summarizes the math at hand.

*Identify shapes with your child using the charts at the end of this book.

Enslow Elementary, an imprint of Enslow Publishers, Inc.

Enslow Elementary® is a registered trademark of Enslow Publishers, Inc.

Library of Congress Cataloging-in-Publication Data
Anderson, Jill, 1968-
  Finding shapes with Sebastian pig and friends: at the museum / written by Jill Anderson ; illustrated by Amy Huntington.
     p. cm. — (Math fun with Sebastian pig and friends!)
  Includes bibliographical references and index.
  Summary: "Review different shapes when Sebastian Pig and his friends go to the museum"—Provided by publisher.
  ISBN-13: 978-0-7660-3363-4
  ISBN-10: 0-7660-3363-5
  1. Shapes—Juvenile literature. 2. Geometry—Juvenile literature. I. Title.
  QA445.5.A63 2009
  516'.15—dc22
                    2008028473

Editorial Direction: Red Line Editorial, Inc.

Printed in the United States of America

10 9 8 7 6 5 4 3 2

Table of Contents

Sebastian Pig loves his new house! But his new room is gray. His friends will help him fix it. They will get ideas at the art museum.

Look at the art with Sebastian. What shapes do you see?

Sebastian's New Room

Sebastian Pig needs help. How can he make his bedroom not look gray?

"Let's go to the art museum. We will get some great ideas!" says Olivia Ostrich.

Circles in the Sky

Sebastian sees a painting he loves. The stars seem to shine right at him!

Sebastian likes to draw stars with points. But these stars are round. "Circles!" Sebastian says. They would look good in his room. So he draws one in his notebook.

Circle

Look at the whole room. What circles do you see?

9

Oval Faces

"Look!" Olivia sees some masks. Some look scary. Some look happy. All of them are ovals.

Sebastian draws some ovals. They look like circles that have been squished.

Ovals

How many ovals can you find?

Simple Squares

"Wow!" Leo says. He likes this painting.

Sebastian does, too. He draws a square.
Are all four sides the same length? Yes!

Square

Can you find all the squares?

14

A Big Rectangle

There is a picture made of cloth. "It's a big rectangle!" Olivia says.

Sebastian draws in his notebook. The cloth has four corners like a square. But its sides are not all the same length. Two sides are long. Two are short.

Rectangles

Can you find more rectangles?

Snowy Triangles

The next room is full of small pictures. Each one has a snowy mountain.

The mountains are triangles! Sebastian draws some in his notebook. What is the trick to triangles? Three straight lines!

Triangles

Find all the triangles!

18

Sphere

Spot all the spheres!

A Silver Sphere

"Come see this!" Leo says. It is a drawing of a hand holding a silver sphere.

Sebastian draws a sphere. He makes sure it looks like a ball.

A Funny Cone

Olivia is laughing. There is a big, soft ice-cream cone.

How will Sebastian draw a cone? First he draws an oval.
Then he adds sides. They slope down into a point. Now he
has a cone.

Cone

What cones do you see?

21

A Tower of Cubes

Will those cubes fall over? No! They only look like they will fall.

Sebastian draws a cube. First he makes a square. Then he draws a few other lines. Now it looks like a box.

Cube

Find more cubes!

Strong Cylinders

A tall building is in the next room. "It looks very old," Sebastian says.

The building has four solid cylinders in front. They are holding up the roof.

Can Sebastian draw one? Yes! His cylinder is shaped like a tube.

Cylinder

Point to all the cylinders!

A Great Pyramid

"Are we in Egypt?" Leo asks.

"I wish!" Sebastian says. He would like to see the real pyramids.

How will he draw a pyramid? It is a square on the bottom. The four sides are triangles. They meet at a point at the top.

Pyramid

How many pyramids can you spot?

28

Can you find these shapes?

Circle   Sphere
Oval   Cone
Square   Cube
Rectangle   Cylinder
Triangle   Pyramid

Surprise!

At Sebastian's house, the friends get to work.

Olivia finds yarn. Leo paints. Sebastian goes into the kitchen.

At last they are done. Sebastian has a surprise. "Thank you for helping me," he says. "I have the best friends!"

Now You Know

Plane Shapes

Some of the shapes Sebastian draws are plane shapes. Plane shapes are flat.

SHAPE	DESCRIPTION	SIDES	CORNERS
Circle	A circle is perfectly round.	1 curved	0
Oval	An oval looks like a squished circle.	1 curved	0
Square	A square has four sides. They are all the same length.	4 straight	4
Rectangle	A rectangle has four sides. Two are long. Two are short.	4 straight	4
Triangle	A triangle has three sides and three corners.	3 straight	3

Solid Shapes

Sebastian also draws solid shapes. Solid shapes stick up from the surface they are sitting on.

SHAPE	DESCRIPTION	SIDES	CORNERS
Sphere	A sphere is shaped like a ball.	1 curved	0
Cone	A cone is round at one end. It slopes into a point.	1 flat and 1 curved	1
Cube	A cube is shaped like a square box.	6 flat	8
Cylinder	A cylinder is shaped like a tube.	2 flat and 1 curved	0
Pyramid	A pyramid is square at the bottom. Its four sides are triangles.	5 flat	5

Words to Know

cone—a solid shape that is round at one end and slopes to a point at the other.
cube—a solid shape that looks like a square box.
cylinder—a solid shape that looks like a tube.
oval—a flat shape that looks like a circle that has been squished.
pyramid—a solid shape that is square on the bottom and has four triangle-shaped sides that meet at a point on the top.
rectangle—a flat shape with two shorter sides and two longer sides.
sphere—a solid shape that looks like a ball.

Learn More

Books

The Metropolitan Museum of Art. *Museum Shapes*.
New York: Little Brown, 2005.

Pluckrose, Henry. *What Shape Is It?* Mankato, Minn.:
Sea-to-Sea, 2007.

Walsh, Ellen Stoll. *Mouse Shapes*. Orlando: Harcourt, 2007.

Web Sites

FunSchool
http://funschool.kaboose.com/arcade/math

KidPort
http://www.kidport.com

Index